Embody
Lent

... in 29 yoga postures

Pauline Steenbergen

Copyright © Pauline Steenbergen 2023

First published 2024 by
Wild Goose Publications
Suite 9, Fairfield
1048 Govan Road, Glasgow G51 4XS, Scotland
A division of Iona Community Trading CIC
Limited Company Reg. No. SC156678
www.ionabooks.com

ISBN 978-1-80432-321-2

Cover image © Ahmad Safarudin | Dreamstime.com
Yoga posture illustrations & self-portrait, Kingswells, 1985 © Pauline Steenbergen

All rights reserved. Apart from the circumstances described below relating to non-commercial use, no part of this publication may be reproduced in any form or by any means, including photocopying or any information storage or retrieval system, without written permission from the publisher via PLSclear.com.

Non-commercial use:
The material in this book may be used non-commercially for worship and group work without written permission from the publisher. If photocopies of sections are made, please make full acknowledgement of the source, and report usage to CLA or other copyright organisation.

Pauline Steenbergen has asserted her right in accordance with the Copyright, Designs and Patents Act, 1988, to be identified as the author of this work.

Bible passages from: Holy Bible, New International Version®, NIV® Copyright ©1973, 1978, 1984, 2011 by Biblica, Inc.® Used by permission.
All rights reserved worldwide.

Overseas distribution
Australia: Willow Connection Pty Ltd, 1/13 Kell Mather Drive, Lennox Head NSW 2478
New Zealand: Pleroma, Higginson Street, Otane 4170, Central Hawkes Bay

Printed in the UK by Page Bros (Norwich) Ltd

Affirmations

Thank you to Wild Goose Publications and editor Sandra Kramer.

Gratitude to my teachers and colleagues in Yoga Scotland, British Wheel of Yoga and Christians Practising Yoga USA.

To all the people I have taught over the years, for so many memorable moments, especially during the 2020-21 Covid-19 pandemic.

Appreciation to the ones in the Diocese of Carlisle, the Northern Mission Centre and the Church of Scotland colleagues who have been so supportive along the way.

Thanks to Steve Blake for his help: www.steveblakephotography.co.uk

To Dad and Ben, thank you for your encouragement and love.

Steve, ever patient husband, your help with the detail of this book has made it better. Thank you for collaborating in the design of the practices and trialling them at home.

Silvie, your friendship since we were 11 years old sustains me more than you'll ever know.

I dedicate *Embody Lent* to my Mum. She grew up in Govan. At age 11 she went to Elder Park Library to choose a book in Adult Fiction for the first time. She chose *Anne of Green Gables* because the author had the same surname as her. Margarete L Montgomery (1942-2020), I affirm the intuitive and courageous choices you made in childhood to end of life. Thank you for teaching me to trust the still small voice in my own body.

Contents

Inhale   8

Intention   9

Self-care   14

Practice   17

Week 1: Ecclesiastes 3 v 1   18

Week 2: Ecclesiastes 3 v 2   27

Week 3: Ecclesiastes 3 v 3   35

Week 4: Ecclesiastes 3 v 4   41

Week 5: Ecclesiastes 3 v 5   48

Palm Sunday: Ecclesiastes 3 v 6   54

Maundy Thursday: Ecclesiastes 3 v 7   60

Good Friday: Ecclesiastes 3 v 8   67

List of postures 1-29   75

Align   77

Expand   79

Holding the space   81

Exhale   83

Inhale

I offer you peace.
I offer you love.
I offer you friendship.
I see your beauty.
I hear your need.
I feel your feelings.
My wisdom flows
from the Highest source.
I salute that source in you.
Let us work together
for unity and love.

Gandhi

Intention

Dear Reader,

All over the UK and in France, a gathering of women and men, representing different ages, genders, sexualities, body shapes, abilities, contexts and Christian denominations, pioneered this material online in 2023. Now I invite you to Embody Lent with me.

At its core, this book is a holistic exploration of Ecclesiastes chapter 3 verses 1-8. These verses are full of universal opposites, paradoxes and dualisms: 'a time to be born and a time to die … a time for love and a time for hate.' The verses intersect well with Lent. This is the season when many Christians focus on Jesus' confrontation with the oppositional forces of good and evil in the desert, as well as his last days leading to his crucifixion. Go to *Align* section on pages 77-78 for Bible references.

There are eight practices, one for each verse, which are suitable to use alone, in a pair or in a group. You will find a list of the 29 postures on pages 75-76. Choose some or all of the suggested postures, breathing exercises, reflections, silent meditations and journaling options. I have offered adaptations for chair yoga where applicable. Use each one of your senses to become as embodied as possible in this experience. Depending on the weather, you might like to take your chair and exercise mat outside. Note that uneven ground, frost, snow, wind, rain, cold air, direct sunlight, birds and insects will affect your concentration, balance and posture. In each practice within this book the movements matter but paying close attention to your breath matters equally. Two years after the birth of my son, I took up running in my spare time. A knee injury led me to a sports physiotherapist. She suggested that I go to yoga classes 'for a good stretch'. My knee healed. The breath awareness which I discovered in those classes was a surprising bonus, giving me a treasure box of tools to manage anxiety and stress. Around the same time a retired vicar and her friend taught me to meditate using a single word mantra, 'Maranatha'. However, it was in my role as a hospice chaplain for children and adults for 5 years that the significance of every single breath and silent prayer truly dawned on me. Years later, when it was our time as a family to witness cancer and death, I will never forget sitting in a cottage hospital praying by my Mum's bedside, watching her every breath until she released her final exhalation. The silence in the room after that breath was the deepest peace I've ever known. My faith is underpinned by a belief that God is the Breath of life. I feel 'yoked' to God's presence when simply I take the time to become conscious of my breath in and my breath out.

The names of the postures are in Sanskrit and English. This acknowledges that the ethos of the postures originates from the Indian subcontinent, pre-dating all world religions. The yogic bends, twists, stretches, inversions, balances, breathing exercises and meditation techniques have evolved from East to West, from culture to culture, practitioner to practitioner, over centuries. Contemporary yoga in the West is now mainstream and accessible for most ethnicities, ages, abilities, genders, sexualities and body shapes; for all faiths and none. It is one modality among many for exploring embodiment. The word yoga means 'yoke' or 'unity'. As a yoga teacher in the UK, I see evidence of this on a weekly basis. Here's an example from my work. Imagine a group of women asylum-seekers from Eritrea, Sudan and Iran, placed together in a North Cumbria hotel – Christians, Muslims, humanists, agnostics and atheists. Their first languages are not English, but the slow simple phrasing, body postures, breath awareness, relaxation exercises and silent meditation by candlelight create an interconnectedness and a channel for Selam, Salaam, Solh, Peace ... which passes all understanding.

Desiring more unity and inclusivity, my stick figure illustrations for the practices are intentionally minimal – four limbs and a head. This is the convention used by many yoga teachers as shorthand when designing class plans. Regrettably, the drawings do not depict every health condition, ability or body shape. Take agency in terms of how you relate to this material. Let who you are and how you feel in your own body be your guide. One practitioner enjoyed modifying these practices for use in a chair. Another person adapted my teaching in a hospital bed, being attentive to his breath, listening to the words read out by his wife and meditating with the suggested prayer word, 'Maranatha'. Being mindful of your unique anatomy and physiology is essential. See more about Self-care on pages 14-16.

Embodiment is a hot word right now, perhaps because most of us exist in physical bodies whilst at the same time living increasingly in a digital reality on phones and online. Social media is potentially changing the way we see our bodies, especially our faces. There can be a forensic overemphasis on perfect bodies, leading to concerning consequences for our mental health.

To me, embodied practices empower us to experience ourselves as subjects rather than objects. Embodiment also enables us to give physical form to words, ideas, images, sounds, relationships – through all our senses. Artists, poets, writers, musicians, actors, dancers and religious worshippers have pioneered embodiment since time began. European Benedictines like Henri Le Saux, Bede Griffiths and John Main were diving into embodied Christian spirituality at least 80 years before me. They were living out a Roman Catholic theological understanding of the body as a sacrament or 'holy mystery'. This view regards the body as more than a fleshy container of air, blood and fluid; it is a temple revealing the Divine presence.

However, attitudes to the body, across all denominations, are not always positive, leading to complex, conflicting and incongruous experiences – made worse by the tidal wave of sexual abuse of children by clergy. Centuries of mind-body dualism have not served us well in the West. 'I am my body/I am not my body' is the splitting paradox with which so many have wrestled, no matter what age, ethnicity, sexuality, gender, body issues or belief system. You are not alone if you struggle to feel at home in your own skin or if some theological perspectives have contributed to body shaming. Feeling at home in our skin can be even more challenging as we grow frailer or if we live with trauma, loss, disability, or life-limiting or life-changing health conditions. Someone I teach has given me permission to share her words. 'At the age of 12 I disconnected from my body and began to hate it. Over the years I have self-harmed, overeaten and become an alcoholic. I have been sober for 14 years now and had a number of years of psychotherapy. Since I started practising yoga things have improved … I still have a long way to go.'

In this book, I teach ways in which you might embody Lent with your whole being, slowly, gently and reflectively. There is no assumption that you have done anything like this before. Where there is a paragraph or two under *Mirroring* this offers some theological reflection. Where there is narrative in italics, these are my personal reflections during the practices. More importantly, there is space for you to pause and mark the text, noting anything that feels positively significant or unusually dissonant for you in your context right now. Embodiment is always personal – set within a context of time, place, culture, relationships and community. This book could become a spiritual, emotional, physical and mental record for you, or you and one other, or in a group, church or network this Lent. Equally it could be used on any day at any time of year.

On a personal level, for half of my life I have been a maker of prayers, sermons and liturgies for worship services, funerals, baptisms, communions, weddings and end of life rituals. Serving Jesus, the 'Word made flesh', is the calling ignited in my teens which continually gives me meaning and purpose. Incarnational theology, feminist theology, liberation theology and eco theology were introduced to me as a Divinity student in New College, Edinburgh in 1991. That's where I encountered members of the Iona Community for the first time.

The Wild Goose Resource Group song 'Christ's is the world in which we move' kept me in the faith when I was disconnected from my own body, broken in spirit and disillusioned by experiences of inequality and abuse of power. That song made a visceral connection in me. It still does. Now that I am older, post-menopause, what anchors me in faith is the hope that embodied practices bring to myself and those I teach. Go to *Expand* on pages 79-80 to find a cross-section of other writings which inspire me and may inspire you too.

Since 2019, inspired by Christine Pickering who founded Maranatha Yoga in Cumbria, I have been pioneering yoga intersected with Christian spirituality. It's a joy to create sequences of movement, breath and stillness, rooted in scripture, for diverse groups of people in a variety of contexts. Most of all it is a profound privilege to hold spaces in which people can share a common search for more wholeness within themselves, with others, with the Earth, with every living thing – and with the Source of our every breath.

Dear reader, who you uniquely are in your body is unknown to me. Thank you for holding this book. It is 'time to hand over' these eight practices to you and 'time to let go' of the outcomes. It is your Embody Lent journey now.

Pauline Steenbergen
Cumbria, 2023

Self-care

Embody Lent is spiral bound to make it easy to use as a practical resource for individuals or groups. Whilst the focus is Lent, it could be used at other times of the year. It was tried and tested in 2023 as a six-week online programme for adult participants across the UK and in France.

For current readers choosing to participate in the breathing exercises, posture work and silent prayer or meditation, please consider your physical and mental-health fitness to do so before you begin. The author is a qualified, insured and accredited Yoga Scotland teacher. She also has a Trauma Informed awareness certificate. According to the gov.uk website, the Office for National Statistics estimated that 3.1 million adults in England and Wales had experienced sexual abuse before the age of 16 (October 2022). Sometimes memories and feelings can be triggered during embodied practices. If need be and you are in the UK, seek frontline support from the Samaritans' confidential helpline 24 hours a day and 365 days a year. Call 116123 for free. Or find a registered British Association of Counselling and Psychotherapy counsellor, www.bacp.co.uk

In the UK or other locations, consult your GP and/or Community Psychiatric Nurse. Seek pastoral support in your faith community as you see fit. You may find a Spiritual Director at www.lcsd.org.uk or www.sdicompanions.org

Each embodied practice is illustrated with stick figures. There is also a narrative description, with cautions and modifications noted. For more detailed advice for practising the 29 named postures see www.yogajournal.com. If you prefer, there is the option to practise seated on a solid upright chair rather than on the floor.

Otherwise, a non-slip exercise mat, bare feet, loose clothing for stretching, and some space around you to move safely and freely, in a warm room or outdoors, are all advised. A solid upright chair can be helpful, in addition to a mat, for seated breathing practices and/or silent prayer or meditation. Listen to your own body, mind and breath – especially if you are hypermobile or pregnant. Avoid doing anything you are unsure of. Give yourself permission to pause, rest or stop whenever you feel the need. Only practise within your range of safe and pain-free movement.

It is recommended that you consider consulting your GP regarding the suitability of undertaking an exercise programme. When participating in any exercise or exercise programme, there is the possibility of sustaining a physical injury. If you engage in this exercise programme, you agree that you do so at your own risk, are voluntarily participating in these activities and take responsibility for all risk of injury to yourself.

It's possible to read this book without practising the embodied sequences. There may be reasons why you can't or don't want to. Perhaps there will be insights and benefits for you through simply learning more about embodiment and how yoga intersects with Jesus-centred spirituality.

The prayer below might mark this beginning:

Optional opening prayer

*Jesus, Son of God,
you were led into the desert by the Spirit
for forty days and forty nights.
At the end, angels came and helped you.
We choose to enter into your embodied experience now
in body, mind and breath.
Maranatha*, Come Lord.*

*The phrase *Marana tha* is made up of two Aramaic words, a language spoken in the time of Jesus. The phrase appears in the New Testament in 1 Corinthians 16:22, meaning 'Come, Lord' or 'The Lord has come'. For many Christians it is an incantation, sounding out the four syllables and sensing Jesus' real presence with us here and now.

You may desire to enter into the eight practices in this book as a preparation for a time of silent prayer or meditation for 10-30 minutes. It may help to set an alarm. There is the option to repeat 'Maranatha' in your mind as a singular focal point, yoked to your breathing, to keep your mind on the presence of Jesus. 'Maranatha' is the prayer word recommended by The World Community of Christian Meditation:
see www.wccm.org
Maranatha Yoga UK also suggests this word as a mantra:
see www.maranathayoga.org.uk

If you have privacy to do so, it can be useful to write down your experiences in a journal to reflect upon, especially if you have felt stirred to action or service to others. If you are working through this book as a group, you may like to discuss your journal entries and reflect upon your experiences together, as long as participants have the choice to opt out if they prefer. Neither the author nor the publisher take responsibility for any outcomes of reading or practising the contents of this book. However, the author welcomes your questions and feedback. See *Holding the Space* on page 81.

Week One

Awareness

I invite you to begin your first practice. You have four options for your initial yoga posture.

Feel free to stand up, taking your awareness first of all to your feet on the ground spaced hip-distance apart and your toes pointing forwards. Then move your awareness to your hands and connect one palm to your belly and place the other palm over your heart. Look softly forwards or close your eyes and observe the subtle sway taking place under your feet, forwards and back, as you stand in this balance which is known as Mountain pose (*Tadasana* in Sanskrit*)*.

Or you can begin by sitting down and back into an upright chair with the soles of your feet planted on the floor hip-distance apart. Gently place the palm of one hand on your belly and your other palm on your heart. Look softly forwards or close your eyes as long as you feel securely stable and steady in your chair.

Perhaps you would rather sit down on the floor cross-legged and upright on your mat. This is called Seated easy pose (*Sukhasana* in Sanskrit). Sitting with your back to the wall, if you prefer, can enable back support and better posture.

Maybe you would like to kneel on your mat instead, known as Thunderbolt or Diamond pose (*Vajrasana* in Sanskrit). Either way, ensure that your lower body is rooted evenly on the floor. A small cushion or supportive padding under your sitting bones can help to tilt your pelvis forwards, raising your hips slightly higher than your knees, lengthening your spine, and making sitting or kneeling more comfortable. Adopt the placement of both hands as suggested for standing or sitting in a chair. Stay in this opening position until you become still. Listen to the sounds around you. Be aware of your space and your whole body in this space. Draw your mind to the natural rhythm of your breathing, in and out. Perhaps you can feel how your hands move in time to each inhalation and exhalation.

Now read Ecclesiastes 3:1-8 in a translation of your choice. The translation below is from the NIV. Hear the words in your mind or read them aloud.

1. *There is a time for everything and a season for every activity under the heavens:*
2. *a time to be born and a time to die, a time to plant and a time to uproot,*
3. *a time to kill and a time to heal, a time to tear down and a time to build,*
4. *a time to weep and a time to laugh, a time to mourn and a time to dance,*
5. *a time to scatter stones and a time to gather them, a time to embrace and a time to refrain from embracing,*
6. *a time to search and a time to give up, a time to keep and a time to throw away,*
7. *a time to tear and a time to mend, a time to be silent and a time to speak,*
8. *a time to love and a time to hate, a time for war and a time for peace.*

Pause. Notice your thoughts and any feelings in your body.

Which word or words connect with you today?

You are invited to embody verse 1:

'There is a time for everything and a season for every activity under the heavens'

Let's begin …

Savasana (Corpse pose)

Sit at ease in an upright chair, soles of your feet planted on the ground. Or lie down on the ground with your back upon your mat, looking upwards. In either position, if possible, move your feet and legs out to the sides, wider than your hips, to the right and the left. Seated in a chair, your knees will still be bent. If lying down, your legs are long and flat on the floor. Gently place the palms of your hands onto your belly, fingertips touching. Breathe in deeply. Notice the way your belly naturally, without effort, lifts and your fingertips move away from each other. Breathe out and observe how your belly lowers and your fingertips reconnect again in the starting position.

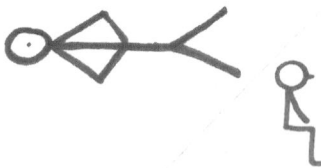

Can you sense how every inhalation and exhalation has its own length and timing? Remember verse 1: *'There is a time for everything and a season for every activity under the heavens.'*

Apanasana (Knees to chest)

Lying on your back or sitting towards the front of your chair, pay attention to one knee at a time. Place both hands around your right knee and stretch your left leg forwards, bringing your left heel to the floor. Lift and hug your right knee towards your belly and chest.

After a minute or less, release your right foot to the floor and take both hands over to your left knee. Stretch your right leg forwards, bringing your right heel to the floor. Lift and hug your left knee towards your belly and chest. After a minute or less, release your left foot to the floor and rest.

Now, only if you are lying down, bend your knees and bring them upwards so that you can place your right hand on your right knee and left hand on your left knee. Bring both bent knees in towards your chest. Cross one ankle over the other. Then in a clockwise direction circle your knees around, say 3 times, and repeat anti-clockwise 3 times. This warms and massages your spinal column against the floor.

If you are in an upright chair, sit in the middle of the chair, place your hands on your lap and gently circle your upper body forward, to the right and back and then left in a clockwise direction, say 3 times, and then in an anti-clockwise direction 3 times.

As we slowly circle our bodies, let us reflect on what it means to be alive on this planet; moving through the cycles of the seasons – Winter, Spring, Summer, Autumn. We become more aware of 60 seconds in a minute, 60 minutes in an hour, 24 hours in a day, 7 days in a week, 365 days in a year ... Like everything that breathes, we are not in control of time or the seasons.

Limbering (Arms and legs)

Lying in *Savasana*, or seated in a chair, inhale and lift up your right hand, arm and shoulder, until elevated to a height that is comfortable. Ideally lift your right arm upwards to the length of a full inhalation. Then gently lower your right hand and arm back to your side on your exhalation. Let this lowering movement last for the whole length of your exhalation. Repeat up to 4 times.

Then shift your attention to your left hand, arm and shoulder and practise the same sequence.

Move your attention to your lower limbs. Do the same practice with your right leg and left leg. You may like to keep your knee bent. Take the time you need without rushing. Can you feel the anatomical connectivity between your lower body and upper body? As one part of you moves, other parts of your body join in, e.g. when you raise your arm your ribs expand. Or when you raise your leg your abdominal muscles contract. Follow the way your breath leads the lifting and lowering of all four of your limbs, like a needle pulling thread.

As you practise flowing movements, perhaps you can more easily sense the flow of nature. Are you able to look out of a window as you practise? Note the season you are in today and how you are feeling in this moment and time.

If lying down, bring your knees to your chest and rock up to a seated position or roll onto your side and ease into the seated pose below.

Dandasana (L-shaped sitting or staff pose)

Sitting on the floor with your spine upright and your feet and legs together straight out in front of you, adopt an L shape. Your knees may be slightly bent. In this rotating yet grounding posture we practise a seated yoga clock. Place opposite hands on opposite shoulders. Slowly circle from your core and pelvic basin, swaying first to the left and then forwards and to the right and back clockwise and then anti-clockwise, once in each direction. Take time to let all your joints join in the fluidity of the movement.

The yoga clock is also possible seated on a chair. Hands on opposite shoulders, simply circle your upper body as above, with your hips, knees and ankle joints at 90 degrees to the floor and the soles of your feet planted securely on the ground.

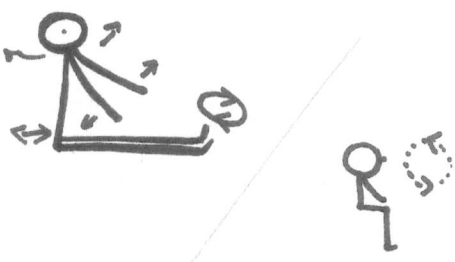

How do the joint rotations feel? As you practise, is your mind like a revolving door, constantly active? Are you aware of any anxieties you may have about time? Too much time in your day or not enough? We may also acknowledge that we have not always understood the timing of events in our lives, e.g illness, loss or trauma. For some of us, this first verse of Ecclesiastes may be challenging. We return to it again: 'There is a time for everything and a season for every activity under the heavens.'

Ardha matsyendrasana (Lord of the fishes)

If you are on the floor in L-shaped sitting, prepare to move into a seated twist. Take your mind to your right leg. Bend your right knee and bring your right leg and foot across your straight left leg. Plant the sole of your right foot on the floor. Flex your left ankle, so that your toes point upwards to the sky. Hug your bent right knee with your bent right arm – in towards your chest. Sit as upright as possible, aware of your spinal column, softly gazing forwards. Breathe in deeply and stretch your left arm and fingers forward at shoulder height. On your next exhale, move your left hand and arm at shoulder height turning left, moving your eyes, head and neck to the left at the same time. Rotate away from the right side of your body as far as is comfortable. Pause and place your left palm on the floor or bend your left elbow and rest the back of your left hand on your spine. Stop when you have turned enough. Hold your body in this twist and breathe in and out slowly and deeply. Fresh oxygen flows into the new spaces now open on your left side. Your inner organs benefit from the detoxing muscular contraction on your right side. Notice the disparity between the right and left sides of your body. Marvel at the physiological unity of every part of your body in this asymmetrical shape.

When ready, on an exhale lift your left hand away from the floor or from behind your back. Level with your shoulder, let your left hand and arm travel slowly back to face forward. Untwist your legs. Bring both knees to your chest and wrap both arms around your knees, giving yourself a hug. Fold your chin forward into the hollow of your throat and make your neck, shoulders and back rounded. This is a counter-pose to your twist. Then uncurl and begin again in L-shaped sitting. Practise the same seated twist on the other side of your body, turning to the right this time. End with a seated self-hug, knees to chest.

If you are seated in the middle of an upright chair, plant the soles of both feet onto the floor. Place your right palm onto your left shoulder. Grip the underside of your chair seat with your left hand. Take a slow deep inhalation. On your exhalation turn your upper body left, moving your eyes, face, head, neck, shoulders, arms, chest, spine and sides of your waist towards the left side of the chair. When you feel ready to stop, pause and hold the twist. Breathe deeply, slowly and evenly. Fresh oxygen flows into the new spaces now open on your left side. Your inner organs benefit from the detoxing muscular contraction on your right side. Notice the disparity between the right and left sides of your body. Marvel at the physiological unity in this asymmetrical body shape. When ready to unwind your twist, exhale slowly, turn from the left side of your chair back to the front of the chair. Give yourself a hug. Take your chin down to the hollow of your throat and make your neck, shoulders and back rounded. This is a counter-pose to your twist.

Then begin again. Place your left palm onto your right shoulder. Grip the underside of your chair with your right hand. Practise the same seated twist towards the right side of your chair. End with a seated self-hug and curl forwards to make your neck, shoulders and back rounded.

Mirroring

During Lent, many Christians read the gospel accounts of Jesus in the desert where he confronted twisty paradoxes, dualisms and oppositional forces.

Looking at the three gospels we can compare different translations (www.biblegateway.com)
Matthew 4:1-11
Mark 1:12,13
Luke 4:1-13

Jesus felt led for a season to turn away from his family, neighbourhood and religious community. Yet he was in intimate communion with God, nature and all living things. In his body he knew harsh heat by day and freezing cold by night. Because he was fasting, he experienced extreme levels of hunger and thirst. Mentally he wrestled with questions, testing, temptation in the form of numerous moral and spiritual dilemmas. The desert was an extreme wilderness for him, with no trees, no shelter – nothing but sand, wild creatures and vast skies. Looking in this rear-view mirror, how do you relate to the embodied Jesus in the world you inhabit now?

Stillness exercise

Our bodies are now warmer, stretched, less restless and ready for silent sitting, kneeling or lying down. Choose the best position for your body now. It's your time to use as you'd like. It could be for a brief minute or longer. Set an alarm. You may wish to repeat a short word or a phrase like one of the mantras below – coming back to it especially when distracted by other thoughts, feelings or sensations in your body. Or use the time to talk to the Jesus of desert solitude. Bring to him your questions, dilemmas or concerns about times or timings which are confusing or need healing. Stay alert enough to connect with what is around you rather than drifting off to sleep. Remain aware of your breathing too. Perhaps you would rather go through your prayer list for others if you have one. Or specifically focus your mind on our planet which is becoming more desert-like due to global warming. Pray for peoples and places affected most by flooding, drought and famine exacerbated by climate change and pray for climate justice. Lighting a candle may be helpful, and you may need to cover up to stay warm.

Mantras

'There is a time for everything'   and/or
'There is a season for every activity under the heavens'

Release

Once your alarm sounds and your practice is completed, note in a journal what your experience was like, with any actions you may wish to take now. If you are exploring this as a group, you might decide to share your journal entry but there is no obligation to do so.

Peace be with you ...

Week Two

Awareness

In a comfortable seated position, on the floor or in a chair, or kneeling, take time to settle your body. With your thinking mind, notice your pattern of inhalation and exhalation. If you need to, take one palm to your heart space and one palm to your belly and take slow, long breaths until you feel calm.

Then read through the scripture below silently or out loud.
Ecclesiastes 3:1-8

1. There is a time for everything and a season
   for every activity under the heavens:
2. *a time to be born and a time to die,*
   a time to plant and a time to uproot,
3. a time to kill and a time to heal,
   a time to tear down and a time to build,
4. a time to weep and a time to laugh,
   a time to mourn and a time to dance,
5. a time to scatter stones and a time to gather them,
   a time to embrace and a time to refrain from embracing,
6. a time to search and a time to give up,
   a time to keep and a time to throw away,
7. a time to tear and a time to mend,
   a time to be silent and a time to speak,
8. a time to love and a time to hate,
   a time for war and a time for peace.

> **Pause. Notice your thoughts and any feelings in your body.**
> Which word or words feel most significant to you today?
> Are there words which have a new importance for you
> as a result of your embodied practice last week?

I imagine that Jesus knew this passage well, even off by heart. In the Hebrew Bible, Ecclesiastes stands between the Song of Solomon and Lamentations. It belongs to five scrolls that are read aloud at various festivals in the Jewish religious year. These eight verses are part of the Wisdom literature which may have been one of many texts sustaining Jesus during the forty days and forty nights in the desert. As an additional challenge, you may wish to learn Ecclesiastes 3:1-8 by heart to recite aloud this Lent.

Let's embody verse 2:
(Please have a long scarf by your side for some of the postures in this session.)

*'A time to be born and a time to die,
a time to plant and a time to uproot'*

Savasana (Corpse pose variation bent legs)

Begin in constructive rest position, lying supine on your mat with knees bent, soles of both feet hip-distance apart on the ground and both palms on your belly.

Or sit in a chair, back upright, with the soles of both feet on a cushion or stool so that your knees are slightly higher than your hips. Feel the way your belly rises and falls as you breathe. This posture is stabilising: it fixes us to the earth and potentially gives us a sense of permanence despite our impermanence. Another dualism! Our breathing is our constant anchor whilst our bodies are ageing and changing moment by moment, as are our thoughts.

Sethi bandha sarvangasana (Pelvic tilts)

Take your mind to the roundedness of your belly, your pelvic basin and your lower back. On your next inhale, feel a micro-lift of your pelvis as you send it forwards, enabling a small arch to form under your lower back. On the exhale, notice how you can roll your pelvis back, flatter towards the floor or the back of the chair. Repeat this practice up to 3 times, matching the tilts forward with your flowing breath in and tilts backward to the flow of air out.

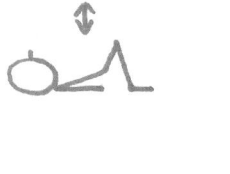 

Here we begin to appreciate where the seeds of a new human life may be sown, planted and grown. Deep in a woman's pelvic basin, a foetus may find a home in her womb-space for up to nine months. We remember the gospel accounts of Jesus' conception, and his mother, Mary – her pregnancy so uniquely poignant at one particular time in history. Focus your attention on your belly button. Recall the date and possibly the time of your own birth. Acknowledge that there is a 'time to be born' for each person. As you tilt to and fro, consider the belief that the timing of our own birth is no random happening. How does that land with you and how does it affect your sense of being here in the world now?

Apanasana (Knees to chest)

In this variation of Child pose, we make our body shape seem smaller and more rounded. If you are lying down, lift your feet off the floor and place the palms of your hands on your knees. Circle your knees clockwise and then anti-clockwise. Then simply hold your bent knees towards your chest.

If seated in a chair, sit further forwards, keeping your feet on the floor and both hands on your knees. Move your upper body around in circular rotations by transferring your weight forwards, to one side, backwards and to the other side.

Together we imagine being born – delivered from the birth canal out into the world. Air hungry, we took our first solo breath, though some of us perhaps needed additional help to arrive and to breathe. A time to be born is a time to be held close to another human body for the first time.

We are mindful that Jesus experienced birthing too, sharing the realities of becoming flesh, incarnated and fully embodied.

Ananda balasana (Happy baby)

If lying down, send both your feet skywards with your knees bent, then take your feet wider than your hips, bend your knees more and slide your hands up towards your shins, ankles or feet and take hold. If possible, sway from side to side.

If you are in a chair, use a long scarf under your insteps, feet wider than your hips, holding the ends of the scarf so that your hands feel connected to your feet on the floor. Contemplate how a baby playfully finds their feet for the first time, and how infants spiral upwards, from lying on their backs, to rolling up to sitting, to crawling and potentially standing on their own two feet.

Jesus was born in Bethlehem. Did Mary and Joseph tell Jesus about the auspicious circumstances surrounding his birth? Did he process the story during his season in the desert? Perhaps he didn't need to be told. In the gospels, some of his teaching suggests clearly that he knew who he was and why he was born. To Christians he is Saviour of the world, Prince of Peace. Spirituality is often defined as the search for meaning and purpose. Why this body and this context? Who am I? Why am I here? What is the purpose of my life?

Viparita karani (Legs elevated)

Please note that this is an inversion posture and may not be suitable if you are pregnant, or have low or high blood pressure or eye problems like glaucoma.

Lying on your back, when you take your next slow deep inhale, bend your knees towards your chest and then lift both of your feet to the sky with knees a little bent, so that your legs are up above your body and you can see your feet. Let your arms rest by your sides or place the palms of your hands behind your thighs to support your legs above you. To come out of the posture, bend your knees and roll onto your side. Take a few slow breaths to recover before using your hands to lift yourself from the floor back to sitting.

You may prefer to be lying on your back with your legs up against a solid wall or resting your calves and feet on the seat of a chair. To come out of the posture, bend your knees closer to your chest and roll over onto your side before moving back to sitting.

If you are seated on a chair, elevate both of your feet and legs onto a chair opposite you. Lower your feet back to the floor when you feel ready to do so.

Mirroring

Back to verse 2: 'A time to die.' This is a harsh statement for any human being to read. Mortality. The end of life. In the desert this was another challenge which Jesus would face. His body, his life, would have been constantly at risk from the extreme elements of scorching sun and freezing nights, hunger, thirst and wild animals. Then, approximately three years after his season in the desert, he would suffer a torturous death, hung for hours on a cross outside the city of Jerusalem like a criminal.

Savasana (Corpse pose)

Seated in a chair or lying flat in *Savasana*, place one hand on your heart-space and one hand on your belly. Feel the movement under both your hands created by your breath in and out. Count your breath IN to the length of 1-2-3 and count 3-2-1 OUT.

'A time to die.' Some yoga teachers encourage their students to adopt Corpse pose at the end of every class. This can be viewed as practising an acceptance that one day our life on earth will end. Do not stay here in this posture if you prefer not to, or if it is triggering. However, if you find it helpful, rest here for 5-20 minutes and breathe slowly and deeply.

Makarasana (Prone rest)

If you are on the floor, roll over onto your front, lying flat. Place one wrist on top of the other under your forehead, with your elbows bent. Take off your glasses or watch if need be. Make sure that there is some space below your face to breathe freely. Your belly, pelvis, hips, the front of your legs and your feet are rooted to the earth. Then take your feet as wide as the mat and allow your heels to roll in towards each other. Or seated in a chair, you could place a large cushion between your chest and your knees and fold forwards, resting your forehead on your wrists, adapting the cushion for support.

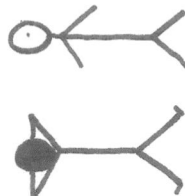

Here in this posture we lower our body as close as possible to the earth. In the universal life-cycle of birth and death, we are connected to every human being, all living things, the Earth, the universe and the source of everything that is.

Back to verse 2: 'A time to plant …' Stay grounded, rooted and planted for a few rounds of slow and even breathing.

Bharmanasana (Table-top pose)

If lying on the floor, release your hands and place them palms down to either side of your chest. Bring your legs and feet together. Breathe in, push up and place yourself securely on your hands and knees. Hands under shoulders and knees under hips. If you wish, sway from side to side and notice your fixed four points of contact with the earth. Honour the symmetry of your anatomy. Your pelvis has risen above the floor, level with your hips and shoulders.

For a chair version, sit astride your chair, facing the back, holding the top corners with your hands and planting your feet into the ground beside the chair feet. Find similar 90 degree angles in your body.

In the desert, Jesus learnt lessons that would plant seeds of wisdom within his body, equipping him for three years of ministry ahead. That ministry in Galilee and Jerusalem was a time when his words and actions would in turn plant seeds of faith, hope and love, peace and justice within everyone who encountered him face to face.

Adho mukha svanasana (Downward-facing dog)

This posture may not suit you if you have any blood pressure issues, if you are pregnant or menstruating heavily, or have eye or digestive problems. It can be left out. However, if you are happy to proceed on the floor, we start in table-top position. Breathe in, turn your toes under, raise your knees off the floor and send your hips sky-high, with your palms and soles still planted on the ground. Your knees will be slightly bent. In this inversion your pelvic basin has been uprooted away from the earth. Feel the blood rush to your brain as you look at the earth upside down. You are heart over head.

An alternative to being upside down on the floor would be to stand behind your chair. Hold the back of the chair on each side equally and take steps slowly walking away from the chair, until your arms are straighter. Fold your head forwards until it is level with your heart, bending your knees accordingly so as to feel a long stretch down your spine. Pause in this position as long as it is comfortable and breathe deeply and slowly. Then walk your feet forwards towards your chair and bring your head up slowly until you are standing again behind your chair.

Here we play with the opposites in verse 2 – planting and uprooting. Jesus was a nomad in the desert, and he would carry this experience with him into his ministry as a Galilean wanderer. The Son of God had no home of

his own, no permanent abode, moving from place to place to teach and heal. Reflect on your own needs. Do you prefer the table-top stability or the more upside-down view? Perhaps you like both for various reasons. We come back to a dualism again, permanence and impermanence.

Bharmanasana (Table-top pose) to sitting

Move from upside down Downward-facing dog onto your hands and knees, to the floor, seated, kneeling or lying down, or sitting on a chair.

Stillness exercise

Now that our bodies are warmer and stretched, let's move into a time of silence. Remember, it's your time to use as you'd like. You may wish to repeat a short mantra like 'Maranatha', inviting Jesus into your embodied experience. You may prefer another prayer word or phrase. Come back to your mantra, especially when distracted by other thoughts, feelings or sensations in your body. Pay attention to your breath. Or use the time to pray for others in the world or for yourself. Perhaps pray for pregnant mothers in labour, midwives, newborns and their families. Maybe you feel moved to pray for those who are at the end of their lives or those who will take their final breath today and those who will be affected most by those endings. Pray for those who are planters, whose livelihoods are the soil. Pray for those who are refugees and asylum-seekers. For those of all ages uprooted by famine, poverty, war, persecution, racial injustice or prejudice. Light a candle for them if you wish, and cover up to keep warm. As today's verses may be triggering, seek the presence of Jesus, the Comforter. Afterwards, talk to someone you trust who can listen well. See Self-care on pages 14-16.

Mantras:

'A time to be born and a time to die'
'A time to plant and a time to uproot'

Release

Once your practice is completed, you might like to note what your experience in silence was like, any actions you wish to take now, and what support you might need.

Peace be with you ...

Week Three

Awareness

Tadasana (Mountain pose) is our first posture. Standing indoors or outdoors, perhaps with a wall nearby, or close to an upright bench or chair, plant the whole surface area of each sole, right foot and left foot, on the earth, barefoot if possible. Take time to feel the subtle sway forwards and backwards, from your heels to your toes. You are balancing your entire body weight on your soles. If you prefer, sit down and back in an upright chair and sink your attention into the soles of your feet.

This posture can be rooting, fixing us between earth and sky, giving us a sense of permanence, which is balancing when we are aware of impermanence. Find your breath by raising your shoulders, bending your elbows and placing your fingers on your front ribs. Locate your thumbs just around the back of your ribs on each side. Feel the expansion of your ribs to your right and left.

Our breathing is our constant reality. The word for breath in Hebrew is 'Ruah', in Greek 'Pneuma', in Sanskrit 'Prana', and in Chinese 'Qi'. Each one of these words also means life-force, energy, Spirit. Consciously breathe in awe as you sense the breath of life within you and the Source of all breath flowing through you. Scan the spaces, objects and beings in your sightline and sense your connectedness with everything that breathes.

Read Ecclesiastes 3:1-8 aloud, or recite off by heart:

1. There is a time for everything and a season
   for every activity under the heavens:
2. a time to be born and a time to die,
   a time to plant and a time to uproot,

3 *a time to kill and a time to heal,*
   a time to tear down and a time to build,
4 *a time to weep and a time to laugh,*
   a time to mourn and a time to dance,
5 *a time to scatter stones and a time to gather them,*
   a time to embrace and a time to refrain from embracing,
6 *a time to search and a time to give up,*
   a time to keep and a time to throw away,
7 *a time to tear and a time to mend,*
   a time to be silent and a time to speak,
8 *a time to love and a time to hate,*
   a time for war and a time for peace.

> **Pause. Notice your thoughts and any feelings in your body.**
> Which word or words lodge in your mind and body today?

Let's embody verse 3: 'A time to kill and a time to heal, a time to tear down and a time to build.'

In this practice, we will integrate that verse above with Matthew 4:4-22 which records Jesus' desert experiences as he confronts the oppositional forces of good and evil.

Tadasana (Mountain pose)

Remain standing, mindful of your balance. Or sit in an upright chair. Maintain an ongoing awareness of your breathing. During Lent, Christians remember Jesus standing in two places: a) on the highest point of the Temple in Jerusalem and b) on a high mountain. It is written that he was tested and tempted to his limits by the embodiment of evil, called the Devil. Jesus, in all his humanity, was standing on great heights at peril from harm, injury and possible death. In these moments he experienced 'a time to kill'.

Utthita tadasana (Angel or star pose)

Stand with your feet wider than your hips and turn your feet diagonally outwards, planting them into the ground, so as to stand balanced and stable. Raise your hands and arms wide, lifting your shoulders until you are in a comfortable, diagonal star-shaped stretch. Hold the posture and breathe deeply into the expansion of your whole body and all the space around you and within you. Slowly, on an exhale, lower your hands back to your sides and walk your feet back to hip-distance, until you are standing again in Mountain pose.

If sitting down and back in a chair, take your feet out wider than your hips, turning your toes outwards. Raise your hands and arms wide, lifting your shoulders until you are in a comfortable, diagonal star-shaped stretch. Hold the posture and breathe deeply into the expansion of your whole body and all the space around you and within you. Slowly, on an exhale, lower your hands back to your sides and walk your feet back to hip-distance, until you return to the starting position.

Mirroring

We learn in Matthew 4:4-22 that, for Jesus, the tug-of-war between good and evil was so impactful – physically, emotionally, spiritually and mentally – that at the end of the 40-day period angels were sent to help him.

> *This strikes a chord with me, that even Jesus needed to accept help, support, comfort and care at times. Like all of us, he needed 'time to heal'.*

Uttanasana (Forward fold)

Be mindful of any health condition which prevents taking your head forwards and downwards.

From standing, inhale and then as you exhale roll down towards the earth, beginning with your chin folding towards the hollow of your throat, then rounding the back of your neck and shoulders and gradually rolling downwards until your upper body is opposite the front of your legs with, perhaps, your fingertips or palms touching the floor and your knees bent. Pause here breathing slowly and deeply.

If you are in a chair, adapt this rolling forwards motion with your palms on your thighs and your upper body folding towards your legs. Sense how this physical movement mirrors verse 3 – 'A time to tear down.'

Phalakasana (Plank pose) (No chair option)

From standing, bend your knees and ease downwards onto your hands and knees. Looking beyond your hands, try to lengthen one leg at a time until the toes of both feet are pressing into the earth and you are holding the long semi-horizontal line of your spine flat with your pelvis, hips and chest in alignment. Or practise half-planks, holding one leg at a time extended to the back of the mat, with your other knee on the floor. What a posture of stamina, endurance, heat and strength!

Every part of your musculoskeletal system is involved. Here we mirror the words from verse 3: 'A time to build.' Bone upon bone, plank upon plank, you are constructing a solid dwelling place with your body. From here, move back to hands and knees. Repeat if you enjoyed building that posture.

Bharmanasana (Table-top pose)

Move your knees down to the floor, hip-distance apart, with the front of your feet flat on the floor and the palms of your hands flat on the ground too – shoulder-distance apart. Your spine is in a horizontal line. If you are seated in a chair, root the soles of your feet into the ground and hold the sides of the seat to help you to honour the 90-degree angles of table-top pose without getting onto the floor. Pause and breathe slowly and evenly.

Mirroring

This posture reminds us that, after his time of harsh temptation and testing, Jesus leaves his desert solitude and re-enters community life. In Galilee we find him fully embodied, dwelling amongst diverse people, eating and drinking with them, going to a wedding, worshipping in synagogues, healing, teaching and preaching in large crowds, on lakes, climbing mountains to pray and living everyday life with his disciples and followers of all ages.

Stillness exercise

Now, seated in a chair or on the mat, or kneeling, or lying in the relaxation posture *Savasana* (Corpse pose), let's move into a time of silence. Pay close attention to your breath. It's your time to use as you'd like. You might want to set a timer. You may wish to repeat a short invitational mantra, like 'Maranatha' meaning 'Come, Lord'. Or use the time to pray for others in the world or for yourself, especially where violence, killing or acts of terror have been involved. Pray for those who are therapists, healers, care professionals and for those in social care, law enforcers, politicians and governments. Pray for the rebuilding of lives and communities. Light a candle if you wish, and cover up to keep warm. As today's verses may be triggering, seek the presence of Jesus, our Comforter and make time to speak to people you can trust for support if you need to.

Mantras:

'A time to kill and a time to heal'
'A time to tear down and a time to build'

Release

Once your alarm sounds and your practice is completed, you might like to note in a journal what your experience was like, with any actions you may wish to take now. If you are exploring this as a group, you might decide to share your journal entry but there is no obligation to do so.

Peace be with you ...

Week Four

Awareness

Sukhasana (Seated easy pose)

Sit in an upright chair, or on the floor cross-legged. You might prefer to sit with a wall behind you, or back-to-back with a partner. A cushion under your sitting bones can tilt your pelvis forward to ease tension in this area. Originally, yoga practices, predating all world religions, were a preparation for seated meditation postures like this one. With your thinking mind, become aware of your natural breathing pattern. Bend your elbows and take one wrist in front of the other one at your pulse points with your thumbs side-by-side and your palms facing you.

Place this hand gesture on your sternum over your heart centre. This is known as Eagle mudra or Garuda mudra. It can be soothing for anxiety and may reduce stress. The hand lock, combined with slow, deep breaths, has been known to help some people feel as if they are held by kind, protective wings.

Recite off by heart or read the verses below, aloud or silently.

Ecclesiastes 3:1-8

1. There is a time for everything and a season
   for every activity under the heavens:
2. a time to be born and a time to die,
   a time to plant and a time to uproot,

³ a time to kill and a time to heal,
  a time to tear down and a time to build,
⁴ *a time to weep and a time to laugh,*
  a time to mourn and a time to dance,
⁵ a time to scatter stones and a time to gather them,
  a time to embrace and a time to refrain from embracing,
⁶ a time to search and a time to give up,
  a time to keep and a time to throw away,
⁷ a time to tear and a time to mend,
  a time to be silent and a time to speak,
⁸ a time to love and a time to hate,
  a time for war and a time for peace.

Pause. Notice your thoughts and any feelings in your body.
Which word or words connect with you or feel dissonant today?

Let's embody verse 4:

'A time to weep and a time to laugh,
a time to mourn and a time to dance,'

In this practice, we reflect on how Jesus experienced so many familiar human emotions. During his ministry in Galilee, Jesus wept when a close friend of his died. He expressed anger verbally and physically turned over tables in the Temple. He revealed existential angst and spiritual distress as he was suffering on the cross, praying to God 'Why have you abandoned me?' In a popular hymn Jesus is called 'the Lord of the dance …' He attended a wedding and turned water into wine. Celebrating milestones, he would have laughed and danced just like us.

Nadi shodhana (Alternate nostril breathing)

Seated upright, become aware of the air in your nostrils. Take the index finger of your right hand and close off your right nostril. Breathe deeply and evenly in and out through your left nostril only. Then take your right finger away and place your left index finger gently against the left nostril and breathe deeply and evenly in and out through the right nostril. Repeat up to 5 times on each side. Complete the practice by taking both hands away and resting them, palms upward, on your legs. Breathe in and out slowly through both nostrils.

Ecclesiastes 3 verse 4 swings from one deep human emotion to the next, seemingly alternating contrasting human experiences. Yet there is a pendulum flow, a repeating rhythm that we resonate with again and again.

Bharmanasana (Table-top clock)

Position yourself on the floor on your hands and knees. Take your mind to your right hand, breathing in. Then breathe out, moving your body-weight to the right knee. Breathe in moving round to your left knee and breathe out as you move forwards to your left hand. Repeat these rotations full circle around your body 3 times, coordinating breath and movement. Then repeat in an anti-clockwise rotation x3. Let your breath flow in and out as you move around clockwise and then anti-clockwise as you prepare to embody more timeless wisdom.

If you are seated in a chair, place your palms on your knees and practise circling your upper body clockwise and anti-clockwise in tune with your breath.

Upavishati balasana (Seated child pose)

'A time to weep.'
We sit hugging our knees, head low, chin towards our heart – vulnerable. 'Jesus wept' just like all of us. Take all the time you need here.

Ananda balasana (Happy baby)

'A time to laugh'.
This might be a playful, fun posture for you and a celebration of joyful innocence and vitality.

If you are seated on the floor, roll onto your back with your belly facing upwards to the sky, heart open and ribs wide. Lift your feet upwards towards the sky with your knees bent. Reach each hand to either your shin, ankle or toes and hold. Sway from your right side to your left side and your left side to right side.

If you are seated in a chair, slip a long scarf under both your insteps and, holding the ends of the scarf, make a connection from hands to feet on the floor. Sway right to left and left to right.

Dharmikasana (Ancestral worship pose)

'A time to mourn.'
If you are lying down, move onto your hands and knees, then ease your sitting bones towards your heels and with your arms parallel, palms downwards, reach forwards. You might have capacity to rest your brow on the mat.

If seated, fold slightly forwards and reach your hands downwards. Drop your chin to the hollow of your throat.

This mournful pose is a reality our ancestors knew before us. The dualism in verse 4 is the stuff of all human existence: the emotional pendulum that swings at any moment from joy to sorrow, affecting us mentally, physically and spiritually.

Dharmikasana, Bharmanasana, Uttanasana, Tadasana
(Ancestral worship, Table-top, Forward fold, Mountain)

If you need a reminder of these four postures then look back through the book. Practise each one slowly in a sequence from the ground to standing. You may like to repeat the sequence in reverse.

In a chair, simply move upwards very slowly from sitting to standing. Observe how you feel as you transition from the ground upwards, moving through the different positions. Embody the cycle of grieving and recovering and accepting. Complete this sequence by standing and balancing in Mountain pose.

Natarajasana (Dancer pose) (No chair option)

'A time to dance.'
There can be joy, celebration and delight in this back-bending balance pose. Every shape, posture and breath you have taken so far in this session will enable this posture to be what it is. Begin by standing in Mountain pose. Find a point of focus for your gaze to help you stay as balanced as you can. Transfer your weight onto your left leg and bring your right leg forwards, bend your right knee and move it backwards until both knees are together and your right foot is behind you. Reach your right arm forwards at shoulder height. Then on an exhale, take your right hand and arm behind you in

order to clasp your right foot with your right hand. You may need to hold on to a chair or wall with your left hand to stabilise yourself. Your abdominal muscles are drawn in and your back is slightly arched. Perhaps now you can hold your left arm straight out in front of you. Alternatively, continue to hold the back of a chair or touch a wall to help you balance. Now fold your head and upper body downwards a little, towards the earth, lifting your right hand and clasped foot up towards the sky. Hold, relax, and breathe slowly and evenly. You are in Dancer pose! Slowly release the pose and ease upwards to standing again. Have a shake out and then repeat on the other side of your body: begin standing in Mountain pose and then transfer your weight onto your right leg etc.

Then transition from standing to sitting or lying on the floor to honour the ongoing flowing cycle of human emotions ... Move gradually by rolling downwards into a forward fold, to table-top, to seated or kneeling and finally lying down. Or simply sit back on your chair.

Stillness exercise

So, now that our bodies are warmer following that embodied practice, let's move into a time of silence. It's your time to use as you'd like. You may wish to repeat the Eagle mudra recommended at the very start of the session and spend some time observing your breath and feeling held by kind wings. You may like to chant a short mantra like 'Maranatha', 'Come, Lord Jesus'. Or use the time to pray for others in the world or for yourself. Today, focus your prayerful attention on one person by name or one place by name. Light a candle, perhaps, and cover up to keep warm. As today's verses may be triggering, seek the presence of Jesus, our Comforter – who also wept, laughed, mourned and danced.

 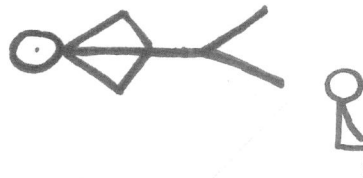

Mantras:

'A time to weep and a time to laugh'
'A time to mourn and a time to dance'

Release

Once your practice is completed, make a note of what the experience was like and any actions you wish to take now. If you are exploring this as a group, you might decide to share your journal entry but there is no obligation to do so.

Peace be with you ...

Week Five

Awareness

Begin standing in *Tadasana* (Mountain pose) or sit in an upright chair. You might like to take opposite hands to opposite shoulders, creating a crossing over your heart-space. Take some slow, long breaths in and out, with your eyes softly closed or gazing at an object like a pebble, stone or brick.

Bring your mind to the verses below. Jesus would have known these verses and lived by wise words like these. Possibly you are feeling more and more familiar with the verses now, too. Recite them off by heart, either in your mind or aloud, or read them.

Ecclesiastes 3:1-8

1. There is a time for everything and a season
   for every activity under the heavens:
2. a time to be born and a time to die,
   a time to plant and a time to uproot,
3. a time to kill and a time to heal,
   a time to tear down and a time to build,
4. a time to weep and a time to laugh,
   a time to mourn and a time to dance,
5. *a time to scatter stones and a time to gather them,*
   a time to embrace and a time to refrain from embracing,
6. a time to search and a time to give up,
   a time to keep and a time to throw away,
7. a time to tear and a time to mend,
   a time to be silent and a time to speak,
8. a time to love and a time to hate,
   a time for war and a time for peace.

Pause. Notice your thoughts and any feelings in your body.
Which word or words resonate with you today?

Let's embody verse 5:

'A time to scatter stones and a time to gather them,
a time to embrace and a time to turn away'

> *What if we interpreted verse 5 as being about boundaries? Boundaries which may be cultural and geographical but also sexual, emotional, spiritual, mental and physical?*
>
> *If we scatter stones, then we pave the way to expanding our walls, dwellings, roads, circles and territory. This might let others in. If we gather stones, we may be doing so in order to reinforce our existing walls, perhaps building them higher and stronger, defensively fortifying our personal space so that we have more safety or privacy, or to prepare against being attacked.*
>
> *When we embrace, we are opening ourselves up, face-to-face, with arms wide, to connect heart-to-heart with another human being. If we turn away from an embrace or physical contact, then we are setting very different boundaries and making it clear that we want to be alone, or need space, or are afraid, or do not trust the person in front of us. We have the right to make ourselves safer. In these verses we see the power of having agency.*

Mirroring

What could verse 5 mean in relation to Jesus in the desert, his sense of boundaries and the time we know as Lent?

In the desert, Jesus was preparing himself to start a ministry which would challenge the religious order of his day. He would develop a group of disciples to pioneer a new way (the seeds of what we know now as Christianity). He would scatter the religious elite and the moral hypocrites with his searing criticisms. Gathering ordinary folk like fishermen, tax collectors, women, men, and the misfits and outcasts, he would set very different and unique boundaries, with new rules about who was 'in' and who was 'out'. Equally, in the desert, Jesus was very clear with the force of evil about spiritual boundaries. He did not perform miracles on demand to prove who he was. The son of God was no show pony, but humbly and authentically modelled in his own body and being how we might live a better way.

Tadasana (Mountain pose)

Standing tall or sitting tall in a chair, become aware of your breathing and balance.

Viloma breath (Viloma means 'against the grain')

'A time to scatter stones.'
Standing, or sitting in a chair, with your arms by your sides, breathe in and take both arms out in front of you to belly height, palms facing each other. Breathe out.

Breathe in again, while you lift your hands and arms to chest height. Breathe out.

Breathe in again, bringing your hands and arms to nostril height. Then exhale audibly, whilst folding forwards, dropping your hands and arms downwards, bending your knees, into a fuller forward fold, swinging your hands and arms behind you. Then slowly breathe in and lift your hands and arms forward and roll up to your starting position, with your arms by your sides.

Repeat this breathing exercise and body warm-up 3 times or more.

On the exhale downwards, imagine scattering and dropping stones to the earth from a great height. You may have a visceral sensation of 'letting go'.

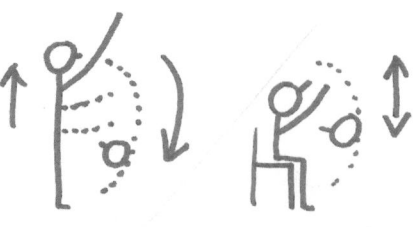

Uttanasana (Forward fold)

'A time to gather them.'

Standing or sitting, slowly roll towards the earth on an exhale, forward-folding over your hip joints with knees bent, and take opposite hands to hold opposite elbows. You may have a visceral sensation of collecting or gathering. Sway from left to right and right to left.

Tadasana (Mountain pose)

'A time to embrace.'

Slowly uncurl and roll upwards on an inhale with knees bent until you are back in Mountain pose or sitting upright in your chair. With opposite hands on opposite shoulders, hug yourself and hold for at least 30 seconds as you breathe in and out calmly and deeply.

Katichakrasana (Standing twist lunge)

'A time to refrain from embracing.'

If sitting in a chair, practise rotating your upper body to the left on an exhale, pausing and staying there with steady even breaths and then exhale as you twist back to centre. Repeat on the right side.

If you are standing in Mountain pose, take your hands to your heart centre in prayer mudra, with your palms together. Step your right foot back and bend your left knee in alignment with your left ankle. Steady yourself with your breath. On an exhale twist to the right side – away from your left knee – and fold forwards to rest your left elbow on the inside of your bent left knee, keeping your palms together and your right elbow up towards the sky. On another exhale, rotate your head and neck to look further round and up to the right side of your space. Pause here and breathe into this 'turning away'.

On an exhale turn back to centre and raise your upper body, whilst stepping your right foot forwards to join your left foot, and release your hands out of prayer mudra. Shake and reset into Mountain pose with prayer mudra and repeat the twist to the other side with your right foot forward this time.

Stillness exercise

So, now that our bodies are warmer following our practice, let's move into a time of silent sitting, kneeling or lying. It's your time to use as you'd like. You may wish to repeat a short invitational mantra like 'Maranatha' meaning 'Come, Lord'. Simply, this means filling your mind with this short phrase, repeating it internally, sounding out the syllables and coming back to it especially when distracted by other thoughts, feelings or sensations in your body. Pay close attention to your breath. Or use the time to pray for yourself or others, or for the Earth. Be mindful of this session's theme about boundaries. Who or what comes to mind now as you enter a time to pray? Light a candle if you wish, and cover up to keep warm. As today's verses may be triggering, seek the presence of Jesus and identify a trusted person to talk to. See pages 14-16 for signposting to support.

Mantras:

'A time to scatter stones and a time to gather them'
'A time to embrace and a time to refrain from embracing'

Release

Once your alarm sounds and your practice is completed, note what your experience was like in a journal with any actions you may wish to take now. If you are exploring this as a group, you might decide to share your journal entry but there is no obligation to do so.

Peace be with you ...

Palm Sunday
The beginning of Holy Week

Begin in **Sukhasana** (Seated easy pose) on the floor or seated in an upright chair, or adopt a kneeling posture. Choose one of the breathing exercises that you have already enjoyed practising in this book, e.g. hands to belly, a crossing over your heart space, or breathing in to the count of 1-2-3 and out 3-2-1, or alternate nostril breathing. If you have a palm cross, you might like to use this as a soft focal point for your eyes whilst you breathe.

Ecclesiastes 3:1-8

1. There is a time for everything and a season for every activity under the heavens:
2. a time to be born and a time to die,
a time to plant and a time to uproot,
3. a time to kill and a time to heal,
a time to tear down and a time to build,
4. a time to weep and a time to laugh,
a time to mourn and a time to dance,
5. a time to scatter stones and a time to gather them,
a time to embrace and a time to refrain from embracing,
6. *a time to search and a time to give up,*
a time to keep and a time to throw away,
7. a time to tear and a time to mend,
a time to be silent and a time to speak,
8. a time to love and a time to hate,
a time for war and a time for peace.

Pause. Notice your thoughts and any feelings in your body.
Which word or words feel significant to you today?

Let's embody verse 6:

'A time to search and a time to give up
A time to keep and a time to throw away'

> *My sense is that Ecclesiastes 3:6 on the one hand points to the human capacity to be curious, ask questions and explore possibilities. On the other hand the verse expresses honestly how humans have the ability to be in denial, to doubt and to give up on what is no longer useful or helpful. Sometimes giving up is safer because some thing, place or person may be dangerous and harmful. These dual capacities are vital strategies for survival and coping. There are many interpretations of these timeless words. What is your sense of them?*

Mirroring

It appears that the younger Jesus is a seeker exploring his own identity – 'Who am I?' Can you see any intersections between Ecclesiastes 3:6 and the last week of Jesus' life? In today's practice we will bring to mind some key moments in those days which we call Holy Week. Palm Sunday is the first day of that week. It is recorded that crowds lined the streets of Jerusalem on that day, waving palm branches, greeting Jesus with singing, and calling him 'King'. Those crowds were projecting their expectations and desire for a Messiah upon Jesus in that moment.

Savasana (Corpse pose)

Lying down or seated in an upright chair, arms by your sides, become aware of your breathing. Take slow, long breaths. Make your exhale longer than your inhale. Breathe in 1-2-3 and breathe out 1-2-3-4-5. Calm your breath to calm your body and mind.

Arm and leg limbering

'A time to search.'
Take your mind to your right hand, wrist, elbow and shoulder. On your next inhale, raise your right arm upwards as if reaching, exploring, searching. When the exhale arrives, lower your right arm slowly to the ground. Repeat this sequence x 3. Practise also with the left arm x 3. Move your awareness to your right foot and, on your next inhale, lift your right foot and leg

upwards from your hip joint, bending your knee or keeping your leg straight. This may feel as if you are walking in the air on a slow pilgrimage, to find an answer or to fulfil a quest. Repeat with the left foot and leg x 3.

Be mindful of a) Jesus the young seeker in the wilderness, b) the religious elite who tried to trap the older Jesus with their awkward questions, c) the crowds lining the streets of Jerusalem waving their palm branches, d) the ones in the crowd keen to catch a glimpse of Jesus in the hope he would rescue them from Roman occupation, and d) the ones waiting desperately for a miracle or a healing or to know the meaning of life.

Makarasana (Crocodile)

'A time to give up.'

If lying on your back, roll onto your front now. With your wrists one on top of the other, rest your brow on your top wrist. There will be some space between your face and the floor so that you can breathe slowly and deeply. Place your feet mat-width apart with your toes turned outwards. We embody a posture that brings your pelvis lower to the earth and symbolises a full stop or a crocodile underwater, lying in wait.

This posture does not adapt easily in an upright chair.

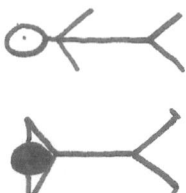

Mirroring

Sometimes human beings stop searching because they have found what they are looking for, but sometimes it is because, exhausted and burnt out, they have given up. This takes our minds from Palm Sunday to Good Friday, when the disciples and followers of Jesus stood at the cross, watching Jesus crucified and dying. This happened in the short space of a week. It takes our minds to Jesus crying out to God on the cross, 'Why, oh why have you abandoned me?' The next day, Holy Saturday, Jesus was lying dead in a tomb. Seemingly a complete full stop and the end of all searching. Jesus, in his inert body in the tomb, expresses the mental, emotional, physical and spiritual pain of 'a time to give up'.

Parighasana (Gate pose)

'A time to keep.'
From lying down, rise up to your hands and knees in table-top position. Take your right foot and leg out wide to the right. Place the sole of your right foot flat on the floor and your right leg straight. Take your mind to your right hand and on an exhale, looking at your hand, turn your head and neck and lift your right arm upwards to a point that is comfortable – as if your body is a gate opening. Notice that, at full extension, your arms are wide in a cross shape. The cross of Jesus opens up the possibility of forgiveness for all, and true unity with God, here and now. Exhaling, bring your right arm down and your right leg, foot and knee back to table-top pose. Repeat the stretch and twist on the other side of your body, using your left foot, leg, knee, arm, hand and side. Breathe deeply, release tension and enjoy the freedom and expansion in this twist, lifting your heart to the sky.

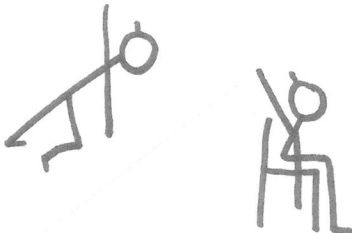

Perhaps you can feel a visceral sensation in your body when holding this cross shape on the right and left? Observe what it's like for you when you are at the intersection between earth and sky.

If you are seated in an upright chair, plant your feet to the floor and lean forwards, lowering your left forearm to rest down on your left thigh. Place your right hand on the right side of your waist. Lean your upper body weight over to the left and inhale slowly, looking at your right hand whilst raising your right arm and shoulder upwards. Exhale as you bring your right hand and arm down to your side. Sit upright again. Then practise this Gate posture in the same way as before on the other side of your body, twisting to the left.

Mirroring

Jesus is called the Gate and the Good Shepherd in the gospels. His death on the cross is seen to be the gate that opens up the way to a personal knowledge of God for all who truly seek. Equally, Jesus the shepherd is always searching for his sheep. The source of all life, the source of our every breath, is constantly beating on the door of our hearts desiring to connect moment by moment with each one of us. Once found, we are kept in this eternal connection forever. Even if sometimes we struggle to feel it or believe it.

Bharmanasana* to *Tadasana (Table-top to Mountain pose)

'A time to throw away.'
From Table-top position, step both your feet up to your hands, with bent knees, transition to a forward fold and then slowly uncurl up to standing.

If you are seated in an upright chair, perhaps you can stand now, behind the chair, holding the back of the chair for support.

Mirroring

Easter Sunday. As you roll up to standing, imagine the rolling away of the stone from the tomb. Jesus is recorded as standing up again in the garden after being laid flat in the tomb. Testimonies say he was alive for Mary in the garden. Alive for Thomas in the upper room. Alive for the disciples on the beach. Alive for Cleopas on the Emmaus road. Death for Jesus is but a comma, not a full stop.

Shake your whole body and being, move every joint and limb and feel the energy inside you move and shift and ignite warmth and heat. 'I have a body/I am not my body.' You may like to expand your limbs further now into Star pose, either standing or seated. See week 3 for a reminder of this posture.

One day, we will be released from these bodies. Be mindful of Jesus who fully inhabited a human body, died and rose again, victor over death, now one with God, source of all breath and life. Many Christians believe that the invisible God is present and real, here and now. How much do you experience God's presence within you at a cellular level? Can you describe in words what that's like?

Stillness exercise

Now that our bodies are warmer following our embodied practice, let's move into a time of silent sitting, kneeling or lying. It's your time to use as you'd like. Pay close attention to your breath. You may wish to repeat a short invitational mantra like 'Maranatha', 'Come, Lord'. Or use the time to pray for the Earth, for others in the world or for yourself. Light a candle if you wish, and cover up to keep warm. If you have a cross you might like to hold it, or if you are outdoors, use a tree as a soft focal point, remembering that Jesus, Word made flesh, who came and lived amongst us, died on a wooden cross, once a tree, and rose again. On Palm Sunday the crowds sang 'Hosanna'. Perhaps this too might be your prayer word today.

Mantras:

'A time to search and a time to give up'
'A time to keep and a time to throw away'

Release

Once your alarm sounds and your practice is completed, note what your experience was like in a journal with any actions you may wish to take now. If you are exploring this as a group, you might decide to share your journal entry but there is no obligation to do so.

Peace be with you ...

Maundy Thursday

Awareness

In a comfortable seated, kneeling or standing position, root both feet into the ground and take some time to become still. Listen to the sounds around you. Be aware of your space. Take your mind to your natural rhythm of breathing, in and out. Today, you may like to have a table near you with some symbols of the Last Supper, e.g. bread and wine or fruit or juice. A yoga block also makes a good communion table!

Ecclesiastes 3:1-8

1 There is a time for everything and a season
   for every activity under the heavens:
2 a time to be born and a time to die,
   a time to plant and a time to uproot,
3 a time to kill and a time to heal,
   a time to tear down and a time to build,
4 a time to weep and a time to laugh,
   a time to mourn and a time to dance,
5 a time to scatter stones and a time to gather them,
   a time to embrace and a time to refrain from embracing,
6 a time to search and a time to give up,
   a time to keep and a time to throw away,
7 *a time to tear and a time to mend,*
   a time to be silent and a time to speak,
8 a time to love and a time to hate,
   a time for war and a time for peace.

**Pause. Notice your thoughts and any feelings in your body.
Which word or words speak to you today?**

Maundy Thursday

Let's embody verse 7:

'A time to tear and a time to mend
A time to be silent and a time to speak'

Bharmanasana (Table-top circles)

'A time to tear.'
On the floor, position yourself on your hands and knees. Take your mind to your right hand, breathing in. Then breathe out, moving your body weight backwards to your right knee. Breathe in, moving across to your left knee and breathe out as you move forwards to your left hand. This is sometimes called box breathing. Repeat this breathing sequence clockwise to the four corners of your body 3 times. Then repeat in an anti-clockwise direction 3 times.

If seated in a chair you may like to sway in circular motions in a clockwise and then anti-clockwise direction, with your palms on your lap, coordinating breath and movement.

Mirroring

On Maundy Thursday, reflect on the supper table in the upper room in Jerusalem. Jesus is with his twelve disciples, including Judas who will betray him and Peter who will deny him. This is their last meal at Passover. Remember how Jesus holds up ordinary bread and wine and makes them extraordinarily symbolic for ever by saying these words: '**This is my body** ... broken for you ... **This is my blood** ... shed for you ...' Here, Jesus is a suffering God, torn and broken by cruel thorns, cruel nails, cruel crucifixion and the cruel spear in his side.

Balasana (Child pose with prayer hands)

From Table-top on the floor, move your sitting bones backwards towards your heels into Child pose. With your forehead on the floor, bend your elbows to rest on the floor either side of your ears and lift your hands, taking your palms behind your neck, so that they press against each other in prayer pose.

If seated in a chair, fold forwards and practise the same prayer hands posture either behind your neck or in front of your chest at your heart centre. Stay focused on your breath in and out.

You may want to remember Jesus in the garden of Gethsemane, after the Last Supper, praying to God to take away his cup of suffering, and how he sweated blood ... how vulnerable, broken and afraid he was: his time to be torn.

Urdhva mukha pasasana (Threading the needle)

'A time to mend.'
This posture is not advisable if you have neck, shoulder, hip or knee issues. From Child pose move your body back to Table-top pose. Take your mind to the space (the needle) under and between your right hand and knee. Slide your left hand, palm down under the space to the right as if to thread the needle. Perhaps now you feel like turning your shoulders, your neck and head towards the right side of your body, exhaling as you twist. This movement brings your left ear and the left side of your head down towards the earth. Balance, breathe and steady yourself there. If you feel able to, take your right foot and leg straight back, stretching until your toes can plant and press down. Possibly you may want to take your right hand and arm upwards, resting your weight mostly on your shoulder, NOT on the side of your head. Pause, breathe slowly and deeply. Press into the floor where your body connects to the earth, whilst balancing in this deep twist. Bring your right hand back to the mat, unthreading your needle slowly and carefully.

Rest in Child pose for a few breaths. Now repeat 'threading the needle' on the opposite side of your body.

If seated upright in a chair, this posture can be practised by taking your feet and legs wider than the chair and adapting the upper body twist above. Place your right hand on your right thigh and lean forwards, twisting to the right and thread your left hand through the space (needle) between your right arm and right leg. Look to the right. Pause, breathe slowly and deeply. Unthread slowly and carefully. Sit upright and begin again twisting across to the left side. Repeat 'threading the needle' on the opposite side of your body.

Sometimes we tear and break, but sometimes we can also be mended, repaired, fixed and healed in this life. Healing is not something I fully understand. But because the gospels tell us that Jesus came back from the grave and showed Thomas the holes in his hands where the nails had been, I am drawn to the suggestion that healing, which is perhaps not always possible on earth, will take place beyond death. In the book of Revelation 21:4 we read: 'There will be an end to crying, mourning, suffering and pain ... the old way of things will pass.'

Bhujangasana (Prone cobra)

'A time to be silent.'

From Table-top pose, move your knees back and your hands forward and lower your body to a prone position, with your elbows bent by your sides and your hands planted either side of your chest. Your brow rests on the earth. Observe your breath as the front of your body relaxes down towards the earth. If seated in a chair, fold forwards over your legs, perhaps holding a cushion or rolled up blanket under your chest and shoulders, with space to breathe.

Mirroring

In the gospel of John chapter 19 we read that Jesus was on trial before Pilate and remained silent at one point. Jesus could have defended and saved himself. He did not answer. When should we be silent, say nothing? Do your times in silent prayer and meditation on the mat or in your chair equip you to practise skilful silence off the mat or chair in everyday life?

Bhujangasana (Raised cobra)

'A time to speak.'
Whilst lying prone, draw your feet and legs close together, squeeze your gluteal (buttock) muscles, press into your palms and breathe in, lifting your chest, neck and face away from the floor, and breathe out through the mouth to hear the sound of your breath flowing outwards. Lower yourself back towards the earth on an exhale and repeat up to 3 times. You can adapt in a forward fold in your chair by lifting away from the cushion as you inhale and moving towards it as you exhale.

Jesus spoke up for victims, the voiceless, the powerless, the broken and the wrongly accused. He spoke loudly against injustice. He died for the least and the lost, crucified between two criminals. He prayed for his torturers, 'Father, forgive them, they do not know what they are doing.' When, where, how and who can we speak up for, and why? During or after any of the practices in this book – have you felt inspired and motivated to take more actions towards justice and peace in the world?

Bharmanasana (Table-top circles)

Position yourself on your hands and knees. Take your mind to your right hand, breathing in. Then breathe out, moving your body-weight back to the right knee. Breathe in, moving round to your left knee and breathe out as you move forwards to your left hand. Repeat these rotations full circle around your body 3 times, coordinating breath and movement. Then repeat in an anti-clockwise rotation x3.

If seated, fold slightly forwards and place your hands on your knees. Circle your upper body, shifting your weight forward, to the side, to the back, to the side and forward again. Coordinate your breath with your movements. Notice that in the chair, you breathe in as you move back and out as you move forwards. Rotate clockwise and then anti-clockwise.

Yoga off the mat is called karma yoga, translated as acts of service. In the circles you move in 'off the mat', where could you be the hands, eyes, ears, feet, heart and words of Jesus today? Who can you speak up for and empower? In Lent some Christians practise almsgiving. This might mean increasing their financial donations to charities or sharing food or belongings with people in need. What could you offer or share this week?

Christ has no body but yours,
no hands, no feet on earth but yours.
Yours are the eyes with which he looks
with compassion on this world.
Yours are the feet with which he walks to do good.
Yours are the hands with which he blesses all the world.
Yours are the hands, yours are the feet.
Yours are the eyes, you are his body.
Christ has no body now but yours,
no hands, no feet on earth but yours.
Yours are the eyes with which he looks
with compassion on this world.
Christ has no body now on earth but yours.

Teresa of Avila (1515–1582)

From Table-top to sitting, move from upside-down to hands to knees and to a seated posture that you prefer on your mat or in a chair. You may like to kneel instead or lie down in *Savasana*.

Stillness exercise

Let's move into a time of silent sitting, kneeling or lying. Pay close attention to your breath. It's your time to use as you'd like. You may wish to repeat a short invitational mantra like 'Maranatha', 'Come, Lord'. Or use the time to pray about inequality on Earth, especially for people, areas and countries trapped in poverty and injustice. Pray for agencies like www.christianaid.org.uk and reflect on how you can take action to be part of the solution. Light a candle if you wish, and cover up to keep warm. Before you begin your silence, if you have symbols of the Lord's Supper, eat and drink them now*, remembering Jesus: 'This is my **body** broken for you. This is my **blood** shed for you.'

Mantras:

'A time to tear and a time to mend'
'A time to be silent and a time to speak'

Release

Once your alarm sounds and your practice is completed, note what your experience was like in a journal with any actions you may wish to take now. If you are exploring this as a group, you might decide to share your journal entry but there is no obligation to do so.

Peace be with you …

---

* *If you would like to see a fuller script for an Embodied Communion, please contact the author through her website. See Holding the Space on page 81. She pioneered an example of Embodied Communion in the outdoors Grove venue at Greenbelt Festival on Sunday 28th August 2022 for an all-age ecumenical group of approximately 91 people.*

Good Friday

Awareness

Begin in *Sukhasana* (Seated easy pose) sitting cross-legged on the floor, seated in an upright chair, in a kneeling position or standing. You might like to take opposite hands to opposite shoulders, creating a crossing over your heart-space. Take some slow, long breaths in and out with your eyes open or softly closed. Perhaps today, Good Friday, you would like to play some music or sing a song or hymn that feels meaningful for you. You might like to clear the space where you are practising so that it feels emptier. You might like to wear something black. Today is our final embodied practice and the end of the period known by Christians as Lent.

Ecclesiastes 3:1-8

One more time, read or recite off by heart all eight verses, aloud or in your mind.

1. There is a time for everything and a season
   for every activity under the heavens:
2. a time to be born and a time to die,
   a time to plant and a time to uproot,
3. a time to kill and a time to heal,
   a time to tear down and a time to build,
4. a time to weep and a time to laugh,
   a time to mourn and a time to dance,
5. a time to scatter stones and a time to gather them,
   a time to embrace and a time to refrain from embracing,
6. a time to search and a time to give up,
   a time to keep and a time to throw away,
7. a time to tear and a time to mend,
   a time to be silent and a time to speak,

8   *a time to love and a time to hate,*
    a time for war and a time for peace.

Pause. Notice your thoughts and any feelings in your body.
Which word or words feel most significant to you today?

Let's embody verse 8:

'A time to love and a time to hate
A time for war and a time for peace'

This is the final verse of the chapter.

Savasana (Corpse pose variation bent legs)

Lying on your back, place the soles of both your feet flat on the mat, hip-distance apart, with your knees upright and your arms and hands by your sides. Settle yourself into the ground. Then take both palms to your belly and feel your breath moving your belly under your hands. Are you able now to feel the 'yoke' – the unity of mind, body and breath?

If using a chair, sit upright with the soles of both feet on a cushion or stool so that your knees are slightly higher than your hips, then place your hands on your belly and breathe into this 'yoke' of mind and body.

You might like to repeat the words below as you breathe:
In you, O God, I live and move and have my being …

Setu bandha sarvangasana (Bridge pose)

'A time to love.'
If seated, sit further forward in your chair and take your arms and hands behind you so that you can hold the back of your chair. Breathe in and arch your chest forwards and upwards away from the back of the chair. This will

lift your belly, open your ribs and incline your chin, nose and eyes to face upwards. Hold your seated version of Bridge pose whilst breathing in and out slowly. To release this posture, bring your eyes, nose and chin back to face forwards. Move your spine to rest back against the chair behind you. Slide your hands onto your lap and sit upright, settling in your seat again.

If lying down in constructive rest position, take your arms and hands close to the sides of your body and your palms flat to the ground. Walk your heels closer to your sitting bones. Continue to keep the back of your head, shoulders, hands and feet rooted to the earth. Then, on an inhalation, lift your sitting bones away from the mat in an upwards motion as high as comfortable so that there is space underneath your back. Your head, shoulder, arms, hands and feet are the supports on the ground for your elevated torso. Roll your back slowly and gently back down to the mat on a full exhalation.

As our bodies make a bridge shape, we are reminded of the role Jesus fulfilled as the bridge between earth and heaven, between what is visible and invisible, between the material and the eternal. See the gospel of John 3:16 – 'God so loved the world that He gave His only Son ... that whoever believes in Him will not perish but have everlasting life.' (NIV)

Adho mukha svanasana (Downward-facing dog)

'A time to hate.'

This posture may not suit you if you have any blood pressure issues, if you are pregnant or menstruating heavily, or have eye problems or digestive problems. It can be left out. However if you are happy to proceed, move from lying on your back on the floor to Table-top position. Breathe in, tuck your toes under and send your hips sky-high, with your palms and the soles of your feet still planted on the ground, and your knees slightly bent. In this inversion your pelvic basin has been uprooted away from the earth. Honour the blood rush to your brain as you look at the earth upside down. You are heart over head.

An alternative would be to stand behind your chair. Hold the back of the chair on each side equally and take steps slowly walking away from the chair, folding forwards to a flat back position, until your arms are straighter, and your head is level with your heart, bending your knees accordingly so as to feel a long stretch down your spine. Pause in this position as long as it is comfortable and breathe deeply and slowly. Walk your feet forwards towards your chair and bring your head up slowly until you are standing again behind your chair.

 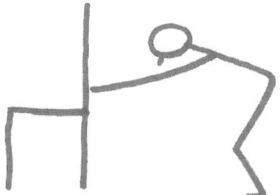

This posture resonates with Jesus' walk to Calvary, how he stumbled and fell under the weight of carrying a wooden cross. Treated like a criminal, a stray dog, he was abandoned, rejected and humiliated.

Next, you might like to read through the following narrative for practising Warrior 1 & 2 and the poses Peaceful warrior and Tree. The 4 postures are practised in full in a sequence with your left foot forwards first, and then repeat all 4 postures in sequence with your right foot forwards.

Virabhadrasana 1 (Warrior 1)

'A time for war.'
If you are inverted, walk your feet towards your hands and bend your knees generously. Slowly roll up to standing. Stand with your feet hip-distance apart in the middle of your mat facing the short edge. Keep your left foot forwards and take your right foot straight back and turn your right foot outwards to a 45-degree angle, so that you are balanced. Your left foot still faces forwards to the short edge of the mat and your left knee is bent in line with your left ankle joint. Your arms are in line with your sides. On the next in-breath, lift both hands and arms forwards and upwards in parallel towards the sky and breathe out once you stop. Hold the shape – breathing in and out slowly. We call this Warrior 1 in yoga.

If you are seated on a chair, only practise the upper body movements, although you might like to take one foot and leg forwards and bend the knee of the other leg so that your foot is under your chair.

Good Friday 71

We are mindful of the times we have harmed others by our thoughts, words or actions and the times we too have been hurt. We are mindful of wars in history, and conflict in the world today. Rarely has there been a time in the world without violence.

Virabhadrasana 2 (Warrior 2)

Still standing in Warrior 1 position with left foot forwards and right foot back, bring both your arms and hands down to shoulder level, holding them in front of you, shoulder width apart. Let your eyes scan along your right arm to your fingers and, on an out-breath, rotate your head, neck, upper body and right arm and shoulder out to the right side of your body until your right arm is behind you. You are still looking at your right hand at this point. Your palms face the floor now. With your arms horizontal, on an exhale turn your head and neck to look down the left arm facing front and gaze along your left arm to your fingers. You are still holding your arms in a horizontal line. This is called Warrior 2 in yoga. It is possible to practise these upper-body movements if seated on a chair. Once you release out of this posture, shake or sway each one of your limbs to ease any tension from the stretch.

In this posture you may wish to confess any sense of wrongdoing or failure. Look to Jesus who died on the cross to take away the sin and suffering of the world. You may like to say aloud, 'Have mercy on me', 'Have mercy on them' and hear Jesus say from the cross, 'My child, you are forgiven', 'They are forgiven' ...

Shanti virabhadrasana (Peaceful warrior)

'A time for peace.'

Standing with your left leg forward and right leg back in the initial Warrior leg position, allow your right arm and hand to drop to your back right leg and rest it there. Look forwards at your left arm and your left hand out front and lift it with your palm facing upwards as you lean back a little. This is known as peaceful warrior in yoga. You may like to say any or all the words you know for Peace as you hold this posture and breathe in calmness. Peace, Shalom, Salaam, Shanti, Myr, Solh. Release the posture. Come back to standing in Mountain pose. If you are practising this in a chair, simply adopt the upper-body movements, holding onto the chair behind you with one hand and lifting your other hand upwards as you lean slightly back in your chair.

You may like to say, 'Jesus, Prince of Peace, make me (us) a channel of your peace, peace that the world cannot give, peace that passes all understanding.'

Vrksasana (Tree pose)

Start by standing in Mountain pose, with a chair or wall (or tree) nearby to help you balance. Now take a few slow breaths and find a loved object in the room on which to focus your attention, or look out of a window at something green and alive. If you are outside, look at a tree. Slowly shift your weight to your left leg. This is your trunk and it's your standing leg. Begin to raise your right foot off the floor by bending your right knee. Externally rotate your right hip joint outwards and draw your gluteal muscles together. Align the sole of your right foot with the inside of your left ankle. Your toes will be pointing downwards and your pelvis will be in a neutral position as you contract your core muscles for stability. Bring one hand to the chair or wall or bring both your hands and palms together into prayer pose at your heart centre. Keep your eyes on your focus. You need vision for balance. If and when you feel balanced, slide the sole of your right foot upwards, either below or above the left knee or resting on the top of your left thigh. Keep your right knee out to the right side of your body. If you feel sufficiently balanced, bring your hands and arms out to the left and right in the shape of a cross.

Here, we embody Jesus on the cross. His cross is a symbol of unconditional love and forgiveness and new beginnings.

Repeat Warrior 1, Warrior 2, Peaceful Warrior and Tree, taking your right foot forward and your left foot back this time around.

Stillness exercise

So, on this Good Friday, now that our bodies are warmer, let's move into a time of silent sitting, kneeling or lying. It's your time to use as you'd like. Pay close attention to your breath. You may wish to repeat a short mantra like 'Maranatha', 'Come, Lord'. Fill your mind with a short phrase or sentence, repeating it and coming back to it especially when distracted by other thoughts, feelings or sensations in your body. Or use the time to pray for peace: for the Earth, for others in the world or for yourself. Light a candle if you wish, and cover up to keep warm.

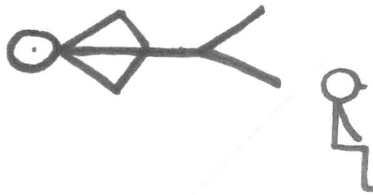

Mantras:

'A time to love and a time to hate'
'A time for war and a time for peace'

Release

Once your alarm sounds and your practice is completed, note what your experience was like in a journal with any actions you may wish to take now. If you are exploring this as a group, you might decide to share your journal entry but there is no obligation to do so.

This moment concludes our eight practices.

Thank you for embodying Lent … and have a meaningful Easter.

> Lead us from Death to Life,
> from Falsehood to Truth.
> Lead us from Despair to Hope,
> from Fear to Trust.
> Lead us from Hate to Love,
> from War to Peace.
> Let Peace fill our hearts, our world, our universe.
> Peace, Peace, Peace.*

---

* First used publicly in July 1981 by Mother Teresa in St James', Piccadilly, London, UK. Adapted from the Upanishads by Satish Kumar. Said each day at noon by people of all faiths and none.

List of Postures

1-29

See www.yogajournal.com for more detailed information and cautions for each posture suggested in this book.

1.	Tadasana	Mountain pose
2.	Sukhasana	Seated easy pose
3.	Vajrasana	Kneeling or diamond pose
4.	Savasana	Corpse pose
5.	Apanasana	Supine knees to chest
6.	Dandasana	L-shaped sitting or staff pose
7.	Ardha matsyendrasana	Seated twist or Half Lord of the fishes pose
8.	Sethi bandha sarvangasana	Pelvic tilts
9.	Ananda balasana	Happy baby pose
10.	Viparita karani	Legs elevated
11.	Makarasana	Crocodile pose
12.	Bharmanasana	Table-top pose
13.	Adho mukha svanasana	Downward-facing dog
14.	Utthita tadasana	Star/Angel pose
15.	Uttanasana	Forward fold
16.	Phalakasana	Plank pose
17.	Upavishati balasana	Seated child pose
18.	Dharmikasana	Ancestral worship pose
19.	Natarajasana	Dancer pose
20.	Namaskar parsvakonasana	Standing prayer twist
21.	Parighasana	Gate pose
22.	Balasana	Child pose with prayer hands
23.	Urdhva mukha pasasana	Thread the needle pose
24.	Bhujangasana	Cobra pose

25. *Setu bandha sarvangasana*   Bridge pose
26. *Virabhadrasana 1*   Warrior 1 pose
27. *Virabhadrasana 2*   Warrior 2 pose
28. *Shanti virabhadrasana*   Peaceful warrior pose
29. *Vrksasana*   Tree pose

Align

Biblical journey through Holy Week

PALM SUNDAY

Jesus and the disciples travel to Jerusalem for Passover and are welcomed by large crowds.

Matthew 21:1-11
Mark 11:1-11
Luke 19:29-48
John 12:12-19

MONDAY

Jesus expresses anger in the Temple in Jerusalem.

Matthew 21:12-17
Mark 11:15-19
Luke 19:45-48
John 2:13-22

TUESDAY

Jesus is in conflict with his religious leaders.

Matthew 21:23-26:5
Mark 11:27-14:2
Luke 20:1-22:2
John 11:45-57

WEDNESDAY

The anointing of Jesus by a woman and the betrayal by Judas.

Matthew 26:6-16
Mark 14:3-11
Luke 22:3-6
John 12:1-8

THURSDAY

The Last Supper. Jesus is arrested. The disciples desert him. Jesus is on trial.

Matthew 26:17-75
Mark 14:12-72
Luke 22:7-62
John 13:1-18:27

FRIDAY

Jesus is questioned by Pilate. The soldiers mock and beat Jesus. The crucifixion and burial in the tomb.

Matthew 27:1-61
Mark 15:1-47
Luke 22:63-23:56
John 18:28-19:42

SATURDAY

The Jewish day of rest. The tomb is guarded.

Matthew 27:62-66
Luke 23:56

EASTER SUNDAY

The tomb is empty. Jesus is alive again and seen by many witnesses.

Matthew 28:1-15
Mark 16:1-10
Luke 24:1-3
John 20:1-20

Expand

A selection of other writings about embodiment and embodied spirituality. Also works by authors writing about the intersection of yoga and Christian spirituality from the 1940s to 2023:

The Wounded Healer, Henri Nouwen, Doubleday, 1979
Women at the Well, Kathleen Fischer, SPCK, 1989
Through Desert Places, Jim Cotter, 1989
What is the New Age Saying to the Church? John Drane, Zondervan, 1991
May I Have This Dance?, Joyce Rupp, Ave Maria Press, 1992
Body of God: An Ecological Theology, Sally McFague, Augsburg Fortress, 1993
'The Bodies of Grown Ups' poem, Janet Morley, in *Celebrating Women*, Ward, Wild, Morley, SPCK, 1995
I am My Body: A Theology of Embodiment, Elisabeth Moltmann-Wendel, Continuum International, 1995
Religion and the Body, Sarah Coakley, Cambridge University Press, 2000
The Forgotten Desert Mothers, Laura Swan, Paulist Press, 2001
Mission-shaped Spirituality, Susan Hope, Church House Publishing, 2006
A Spirituality of Survival, Barbara Glasson, Continuum, 2009
Bodies, Susie Orbach, Profile Books, 2010
Jesus, the Teacher Within, Lawrence Freeman, SCM Press, 2010
Self-Compassion, Kristin Neff, Hodder and Stoughton, 2011
The Body Keeps the Score, Bessel Van Der Kolk, Penguin, 2014
Body, Paula Gooder, SPCK, 2016
Mindfulness and Christian Spirituality, Tim Stead, SPCK, 2016
Wintering, Katherine May, Penguin, 2020
Church of the Wild, Victoria Loorz, Broadleaf Books, 2021
A Plea for Embodied Spirituality: The Role of the Body in Religion, Fraser Watts, SCM, 2022
Sacred Nature, Karen Armstrong, Bodley Head, 2022
Disobedient Bodies, Emma Dabiri, Welcome Collection, 2023
The Hidden Fires, Merryn Glover, Polygon, 2023
Quinn, Em Strang, Oneworld, 2023

*

Christian Yoga, Jean Dechanet, Search Press, 1960
Upanishads, Gita and Bible, Geoffrey Parrinder, Faber and Faber, 1962

Yoga in Ten Lessons, Jean Dechanet, Burns and Oates, 1965
Yoga and God, Jean Dechanet, Search Press, 1974
The Marriage of East and West, Bede Griffiths, Collins, 1976
Sadhana: Christian Exercises in Eastern Form, Anthony de Mello, Doubleday 1984
Awareness, Anthony de Mello, Fount Paperbacks, 1990
Prayer of Heart and Body: Meditation and Yoga as a Christian Spiritual Practice, Thomas Ryan, Paulist Press, 1991
The Cave of the Heart: A Biography of Abhishiktananda, Henri Le Saux, Shirley Du Boulay, Orbis, 2005
The Yoga of Jesus, Paramahansa Yogananda, Self-Realization Fellowship, 2007
Stretching Your Faith: Practicing Postures of Prayer to Create Peace, Balance and Freedom, Michelle Thielen, BookBaby, 2016
Meditative Movements: Christ Centred Yoga with Devotional Prayer, Rie Frilund Skarhoj, Re-source, 2019
Maranatha Yoga, Christine Pickering, Columba Books, 2019
Biblical Yoga, Yvonne Myers, www.mha.org.uk
Jesus in My Practice, Jody Thomae, Amazon, 2021
Voices of Wisdom in the Body, Jody Thomae, Amazon, 2023
Maranatha Yoga UK Foundations Course Manual, Pauline Steenbergen, www.Maranathayoga.org.uk, 2023

Holding the Space

Pauline Steenbergen is an Associate Member of the Iona Community, a Church of Scotland minister in the Presbytery of Southwest Scotland, a Spiritual Director, a self-supporting pioneer with Permission to Officiate in the Diocese of Carlisle and a Yoga Scotland teacher. You will find her on two green mats, intersected in the shape of a cross, in Southwest Scotland, Cumbria and on Zoom. She teaches yoga in village halls, schools, a leisure centre, churches, health care settings, the outdoors, residential retreats, UK-wide events and yoga teacher trainings. Pauline believes that mind-body dualism in any sector is dangerous, but in religious communities it is toxic. 'In our digital age, this is the season for embodiment,' she says. 'The holistic modality of yoga offers a toolbox for more embodied wholeness, unity and peace – moment by moment … Attentiveness to ourselves as autonomous subjects rather than objects can result in more compassion, empathy and wellbeing. For me, Jesus-centred embodiment is the way towards better self-care, and improved relationships with others, the Earth and all living things, as well as deeper intimacy with the Source of all breath.'

If you have questions or feedback about this book, please contact the author via her website: www.limegreenyogi.co.uk

Exhale

Come to me,
all you who are weary and burdened,
and I will give you rest.

Take my yoke upon you and learn from me,
for I am gentle and humble in heart,
and you will find rest for your souls.

For my yoke is easy and my burden is light.

Jesus
Matthew 11:28-30 (NIV)

For notes

For notes

For notes

Wild Goose Publications, the publishing house of the Iona Community established in the Celtic Christian tradition of Saint Columba, produces books, e-books, CDs and digital downloads on:

- holistic spirituality
- social justice
- political and peace issues
- healing
- innovative approaches to worship
- song in worship, including the work of the Wild Goose Resource Group
- material for meditation and reflection

Visit our website at
www.ionabooks.com
for details of all our products and online sales